Pebble™

First Biographies

Abraham Lincoln

by Barbara Knox

Consulting Editor: Gail Saunders-Smith, Ph.D.
Consultant: Thomas F. Schwartz, Ph.D.
Illinois State Historian
Illinois Historic Preservation Agency
Springfield, Illinois

Capstone
press
Mankato, Minnesota

Pebble Books are published by Capstone Press
151 Good Counsel Drive, P.O. Box 669, Mankato, Minnesota 56002
www.capstonepress.com

1 2 3 4 5 6 09 08 07 06 05 04

Library of Congress Cataloging-in-Publication Data
Knox, Barbara.
    Abraham Lincoln / by Barbara Knox.
    p. cm.—(First biographies)
    Summary: A simple biography of the man who served as president of the
United States during the Civil War.
    Includes bibliographical references and index.
    ISBN 0-7368-2086-8 (hardcover)
    1. Lincoln, Abraham, 1809–1865—Juvenile literature. 2. Presidents—United
States—Biography—Juvenile literature. [1. Lincoln, Abraham, 1809–1865.
2. Presidents.] I. Title. II. Series: First biographies (Mankato, Minn.)
E457.905.E44 2004
973.7'092—dc22   2003015822

Note to Parents and Teachers

The First Biographies series supports national history standards for
units on people and culture. This book describes and illustrates the
life of Abraham Lincoln. The photographs support early readers in
understanding the text. This book also introduces early readers to
subject-specific vocabulary words, which are defined in the
Glossary. Early readers may need assistance to read some words
and to use the Table of Contents, Glossary, Read More, Internet
Sites, and Index/Word List sections of the book.

Table of Contents

Time Line

1809
born

4

Early Life

Abraham Lincoln was born in Kentucky in 1809. His family moved to Indiana when Abraham was 7. He did chores and read books.

log cabin where Abraham was born

Time Line

1809
born

1830
moves to
Illinois

At age 21, Abraham moved to Illinois. He worked hard. Abraham ran a store and served as postmaster. He also cut wood for fences.

◄ Abraham cutting wood around 1830

Time Line

1809
born

1830
moves to
Illinois

1842
marries
Mary Todd

Abraham married
Mary Todd in 1842.
They had four sons.
The family lived in
Springfield, Illinois.

◄ Abraham's wife, Mary Todd, around 1846

Time Line

1809
born

1830
moves to
Illinois

1842
marries
Mary Todd

1846
elected to
U.S. Congres-

President Lincoln

After becoming a lawyer, Abraham worked in politics. In 1846, he was elected to the U.S. Congress. Abraham became president in 1861.

1861
becomes
president

Time Line

1809
born

1830
moves to
Illinois

1842
marries
Mary Todd

1846
elected to
U.S. Congress

12

In the 1800s, many people in the South owned slaves. Slaves were not able to choose their jobs or where they lived. Abraham wanted to make slaves free.

◀ slaves working in a sugarcane field in the South

1861
becomes
president

Time Line

1809
born

1830
moves to
Illinois

1842
marries
Mary Todd

1846
elected to
U.S. Congres

The Civil War

The Civil War began
in 1861. The South wanted
to be a separate country.
The North fought against
the South. They fought about
slavery and states' rights.

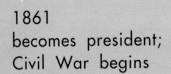

◄ Abraham visiting Civil War soldiers in 1862

1861
becomes president;
Civil War begins

Time Line

1809
born

1830
moves to
Illinois

1842
marries
Mary Todd

1846
elected to
U.S. Congress

16

In 1863, Abraham signed a paper called the Emancipation Proclamation. The paper helped free many slaves. In 1865, the Civil War ended.

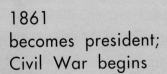
Abraham giving a speech around 1865

1861
becomes president;
Civil War begins

1865
Civil War ends

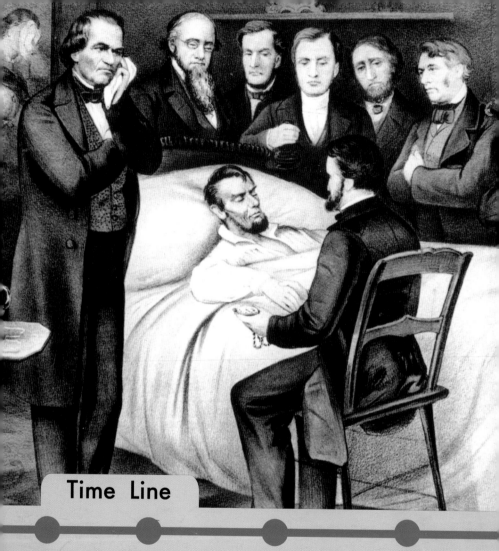

Time Line

1809
born

1830
moves to
Illinois

1842
marries
Mary Todd

1846
elected to
U.S. Congres

Remembering Abraham

Some people did not agree with Abraham's ideas. John Wilkes Booth shot Abraham at a play on April 14, 1865. Abraham died the next morning.

1861
becomes president;
Civil War begins

1865
Civil War ends;
Abraham dies

Time Line

1809
born

1830
moves to
Illinois

1842
marries
Mary Todd

1846
elected to
U.S. Congres

Abraham helped change the United States. He helped end slavery. People remember Abraham Lincoln as a great speaker. He kept the United States together as one country.

1861
becomes president;
Civil War begins

1865
Civil War ends;
Abraham dies

Glossary

Civil War—the U.S. war fought between the Northern states and the Southern states; the Civil War lasted from 1861 to 1865.

Congress—the part of the U.S. government that makes laws

elect—to choose someone by voting

Emancipation Proclamation—an important government paper that helped free slaves; Abraham signed this paper.

lawyer—a person who is trained to advise people about the law; lawyers act and speak for people in court.

politics—the act or science of governing a city, state, or country

slave—a person who is bought and sold as property; slaves are not free to choose their homes or jobs.

states' rights—the rights that states have to make their own laws and rules

Read More

Armentrout, David, and Patricia Armentrout.
Abraham Lincoln. People Who Made a Difference.
Vero Beach, Fla.: Rourke, 2002.

Black, Sonia. *Let's Read about Abraham Lincoln.*
Scholastic First Biographies. New York: Scholastic,
2002.

Internet Sites

FactHound offers a safe, fun way to find Internet sites
related to this book. All of the sites on FactHound
have been researched by our staff.

Here's how:

1. Visit *www.facthound.com*
2. Type in this special code **0736820868** for
   age-appropriate sites. Or enter a search word
   related to this book for a more general search.
3. Click on the **Fetch It** button.

FactHound will fetch the best sites for you!

Index/Word List

Word Count: 214
Early-Intervention Level: 19

Editorial Credits

Mari C. Schuh, editor; Heather Kindseth, cover designer and illustrator;
   Enoch Peterson, production designer; Scott Thoms, photo researcher;
   Karen Risch, product planning editor

Photo Credits

Courtesy of The Lincoln Museum, Fort Wayne, IN (#0-2b), 1
Getty Images/Hulton Archive, cover, 4, 6, 14, 16, 18
Library of Congress, 8, 20
North Wind Picture Archives, 10, 12